YORKSHIRE MILLENNIUM FACT BOOK

GRAEME JOHNSON

Dalesman Publishing Company Ltd
Stable Courtyard, Broughton Hall,
Skipton, North Yorkshire BD23 3AZ

First published 1999

© Dalesman Publishing Company Ltd

Cartoons by The Silvey-Jex Partnership

A British Library Cataloguing in Publication record
is available for this book

ISBN 1 85568 168 4

Printed by Amadeus Press, Huddersfield

CONTENTS

,

WELCOME!

This is the Yorkshire Millennium Fact Book, crammed with all manner of information about the people and places that make this county truly the best in Britain. We have many things to be proud about, whether they relate to historical feats, or sporting glory, or, indeed, anything to do with our wonderful heritage.

So sit back, put your feet up and pour yourself a cuppa (or indeed, something a bit stronger) and prepare to enjoy what will prove to be the ultimate reference book about our fair county.

The flying policeman from Bradford – page 37

HOW IT ALL BEGAN

Those were the days: many thousands of years ago, the first visitors trundled in to Yorkshire, no doubt glad to be able to put down roots after the end of the last Ice Age.

Stone Age hunters were able to cross over from the continent on foot without getting their feet wet, borders were non-existent, unlike today, when pen-pushers seem always to be wanting to shift towns and villages in, and then out, of God's Own County!

Those Romans tried to bring what they thought was a "civilising" influence to us just under 2000 years ago. It should have been the other way round, really, but there you go.

As any true Yorkshireman or woman knows, our County is divided into three Ridings and it was the Vikings gave us this wonderful legacy as the title comes from their word "Thriding" or third. And not a lot of people know that.

York takes the honours for being the oldest city in the County, going by the very grand Roman name of Eboracum, and being founded back in AD71.

And that's about it.

We've been here for ages, and will continue to do so. We're a proud lot — and a friendly lot, with a heritage that many offcumdens (that's none-Yorkshirefolk to latecomers) are genuinely jealous of.

Stone age hunters were able to cross over from the continent on foot...

POTTED GEOGRAPHY LESSON

Most Northerly Place: This honour goes to Holwick in Upper Teesdale.

Most Southerly Place: Take a bow Totley, nestling down near Sheffield.

Most Easterly Place: Kilnsea, Spurn Head — any further and you'd get your feet wet!

Most Westerly Place: Low Bentham, just outside the National Park Boundary.

Highest Mountain: Mickle Fell — 2,591 feet. Climb this to get to know the meaning of "breathtaking".

Longest Water Course: From the source of the River Swale to Spurn Point below Hull is 184 miles.

Highest Waterfall: The beautiful Hardraw Force which plunges 100 feet.

Largest Natural Lake: Take a trip to visit Hornsea Mere on the East Coast.

Largest Forest: The mighty North Riding Forest Park has an area of 12,220 (truly broad) hectares.

Highest Road: Fleet Moss reaches the peak of success here at 1,934 feet, linking Buckden to Hawes. Incidentally, Hawes is the highest market town in England, although some others have had the cheek to challenge this title.

Steepest Road: This is a first gear-crunching effort in the North Riding with a frightening one-in-three climb around Rosedale Bank Top. (That's 33.3 per cent in new money!)

Highest Railway Station: Ribblehead, towering above all others at 1,020 feet. Budding anoraks may like to know that the longest railway platform in Yorkshire is at York Station, measuring 1,692 feet. Oh, it's platform eight, by the way, if you really feel the desire to know that...

Highest Sea-Cliff: Boulby, near Staithes measures up to this one with a dizzying 666 feet under its belt. Not only is it the highest in Yorkshire, but the highest point on any point on the East Coast of England.

Most Inland Port: Would you believe Selby? If you would, you'd be correct, as it is 66 miles from the North Sea. A long way to trek for the old Duty Free.

Deepest Pothole: Have a large intake of breath, and consider this: should you find yourself at the foot of Meregill Hole at Chapel-le-Dale near Ingleton, you would have the more-than-daunting feat of clambering 560 feet to get you back to daylight. Spooky!

Remotest Village: The very quiet Kettleness is six miles from Whitby, and the nearest bus stop is a mile-and-a-half away. Just the sort of place to go to get away from it all.

Highest Inn in England: Tan Hill tops the lot at a staggering 1,732 feet (and you'd probably be staggering too after climbing up to try and catch last orders).

Oldest Inn in England: The delightful Bingley Arms at Bardsey was first used as a watering hole way back in AD905. It's fair to say that the prices will have gone up a fair bit since then!

Oldest School in England: This honour goes to St Peter's in York which first admitted pupils in AD627.

Longest Single-Word Place-Name: Take a really deep breath and go for this one: Sutton-under-Whitestonecliffe in North Yorkshire, which weighs in at an impressive 27 letters. Worth bearing in mind for any future Scrabble games.

Oddest Place-Names: If you ever find yourself in some of our most southernmost villages you may well feel as though you have been drinking when you seen a sign for Wales.

Don't worry, you haven't, it's just a local hamlet. Mind you, speaking of having a pint, there's always the hamlet of Booze in the hills above Langthwaite. Trouble is, it doesn't have a pub.

And talking of having a laugh, there's always Giggleswick, although this has more to do with being named after the a Scandinavian Chief called Gigel than supping Tetley's or Theakstons.

SONS AND DAUGHTERS

Our legacy to the country is a host of people who have shaped the history of far more than the County, but the country itself. Here are some of the most famous ones.

Frederick Delius: 19th century classical music composer, came from Bradford and is remembered there today with a leaf-like statue outside the Crown Court. Was said never to be that fond of the City — off-key, as it were.

Guy Fawkes: Always fond of going out with a bang or two, this (in)famous son of York did his bit for Parliamentary reform with a cunning plot. Incidentally, his old school in York still does not celebrate Guy Fawkes' Night. Was once a church bellringer — honest!

Dick Turpin: Another local lad (Pontefract, actually) with a healthy disrespect for all those in authority (as long as he met them on the highway with plenty of brass on them), Dick came to a grim end after spending his last night in a York prison. Nobody knows what happened to his horse Black Bess though — no truth in the rumour she has been seen being backed in the 3.10 at the local race-course.

Thomas Chippendale: Nothing to do with those chaps that get their clothes off at the first opportunity, but in fact, a mild-mannered cabinet-maker from Otley whose work is now highly prized.

Captain James Cook: A legend with his exploring in the 18th century. A big fan of Whitby.

Thomas Lord: Founder of Lord's cricket ground in London. You would have thought that he would have wanted to be called Thomas Headingley, but 'twas not to be — and he was born at Thirsk in 1755.

J.B.Priestley: Like Delius, a Bradford lad, but in his case it was literature, rather than music, that was to make his name.

Henry Moore: Ground-breaking (and rock-breaking) sculptor who has turned around the appreciation of his art. A Castleford-born individual who never forgot his roots.

Amy Johnson: A true pioneer, showing Yorkshire grit — she flew solo to Australia in the early part of the 20th century. Died tragically early in 1941.

Emily, Anne and Charlotte Brontë: This Tyke trio set the world of literature alight with their stunning contributions. Although it's Haworth that is known as their home, it was at Thornton, near Bradford that the ladies were born. Try that one at your pub quiz.

David Hockney: Painter, stage designer and photographer. Hugely popular painter who has a permanent exhibition at Salts Mill in Saltaire, near Bradford. Well worth a visit if you get the chance. Now lives in California: well, it's his choice!

Alan Bennett: A playwright without peers. Best-known for his television works on the BBC, where a certain Dame Thora has taken some cracking starring roles.

W.H.Auden: You know that poem read out in Four Weddings and a Funeral when the guy with the beard passes away? "Stop all the clocks," etc; well, this chap wrote it, along with many more fine works.

Sean Bean: Rough, tough actor who sets ladies' hearts a-fluttering with his dashing portrayals.

Brian Clough: Probably the best manager that England have never had — and not many people know he's a Yorkshire-gent, although he didn't endear himself too much to the Leeds United fans in the seventies.

Don Revie: Probably the best manager that Leeds United have had. His side's brand of hard-tackling 30-odd years ago won few friends among neutrals (are there such things in football) but made him a true hero at Elland Road.

Fred Trueman: Fiery Fred is probably one of the most famous of our sons with his feats as a Yorkshire and England bowler being admired across the world. Even in Lancashire.

Prince Naseem: One of Sheffield's stars — love him or hate him, he has brought a bit of showmanship — and welcome publicity — to the area. Actually, if you do hate him, don't tell him, for this is one mean boxer.

Jarvis Cocker: Frontman with the group Pulp. Another South Yorkshireman who is not afraid to speak his mind; if in doubt, just ask Michael Jackson at those Brit Awards!

Mel B (Scary Spice): Top Leeds lass who shot to fame with the Spice Girls in their quest for world domination.

Michael Parkinson: Unarguably the greatest television talk-show host ever. Famed for his quizzing of Mohammed Ali, Woody Allen, and, of course, Rod Hull and that "bloody" bird.

Dickie Bird: The world's most famous umpire? Probably. The best ever? Definitely. Our Dickie is as Barnsley as the chop. Advice — always have a handkerchief close at hand when you meet him...

Brian Glover: The late actor personified to many people all the things that being a Yorkshireman meant. If in doubt, just nip down to the video shop and get out a copy of Kes.

John Barry: Excellent film score writer whose greatest hits involved the James Bond themes — he's just been awarded the MBE for his efforts.

INVENTORS AND FIRSTS

Inventor of "Catseyes": On reflection, this honour goes to Percy Shaw of Halifax who must be credited with making our roads so much safer.

First Maker of Liquorice Sweets: For fans of Pontefract Cakes, the man to thank for their invention in 1760 is George Dunhill who was working as a chemist in .... Pontefract — where else?

First Lock, Hydraulic Press and Beer Pump: Ladies and gentlemen, please raise your glasses to one Joseph Bramah of Stainborough who must be the toast of drinkers everywhere.

World's First Man-Carrying Glider: Sir George Cayley of Brompton managed this aeronautical feat in 1853. He was also a pioneer of the aeroplane, hot air engine, caterpillar tractor and airships. However, apart from that he was a bit of a lazybones at heart.

First Man to Discover the Properties of Oxygen: Joseph Priestley, born in Fieldhead, Birstall in 1734, and often referred to as the father of modern chemistry, was responsible for this breathtaking success.

First Woman to Make a "Parachute" Descent: A real odd fact this one, dating back to 1776 when a young lady from Rigton distraught at the ending of a love affair threw herself off Almscliffe Crag. Her skirts then billowed out and she floated safely down to the ground. Don't try this one at home.

First Air Service: The Great Yorkshire Show Airline took off between Leeds and Bradford in 1914. This monoplane was made in Leeds, although the manufacturers went by the un-Tyke name of the Blackburn Aeroplane Company Ltd.

First to use the White Rose as his Emblem: The excellent Richard Plantagenet, Duke of York. What intense good taste.

First Mechanical Woolcombing: This was invented by Samuel Cunliffe Lister, first Baron Masham, who lived from 1815 to 1906. Having worked out that wool could be turned into real brass, he took out 150 patents to make sure nobody could get their hands on his ideas. He also helped make Bradford the wool capital of the world.

First Invention of a Shearing Machine: Enoch and James Taylor managed this, much to the fury of those who had earned their living carrying out the task by hand.

First Discovery of Stainless Steel: Harry Brearley managed this feat in 1913 and did for Sheffield what Lister did for Bradford.

First Yorkshire President of the National Farmers' Union: Sir James Turner (later Lord Netherthorpe), was first elected to this office in 1945 at the age of 37, retiring 14 years later.

Watch the Birdie: Cherry Kearton of Thwaite in Swaledale published the first illustrated ornithological book in the world, and in 1903 took the first motion pictures of a wild bird.

Campaigner for the Anti-Slavery Lobby: William Wilberforce, who became the Tory MP for Hull in 1780 and Yorkshire four years later, took up the cudgels on behalf of those who wanted the trade in humans scrapped. Quite right too.

Founder of the NSPCC: Benjamin Waugh of Settle takes this title, and along with William Wilberforce, it just goes to show what an all-round good bunch we are in Yorkshire.

Designer and Builder of the World's First Steam Locomotive: Matthew Murray got all fired up with ambition after arriving in Leeds without a penny to his name in 1790 and managed this feat.

First Woman to Conduct a Marriage in the Church of England: Deacon Sylvia Mutch helped break the centuries of male domination when she took charge of a wedding service at the Church of St Philip and St James in York on March 18, 1987. Bless her!

YOU WOULDN'T BELIEVE IT

Oldest Man: This (barely credible) record was claimed by Henry Jenkins who assured those who would listen that he had notched up 169 years at Bolton-in-Swale between 1500 and 1670. Obviously there was nobody around to dispute his claims. And the reason for his longevity? The unlikely combination of "the virtues of cold water, raw onions and wearing flannel next to the skin from infancy". It may have worked, but you can't exactly see it catching on.

Oldest Bride: Mrs Winifred Clark who married at Cantley in South Yorkshire in 1971 was one day short of her 100th birthday. Her toyboy bridegroom was a mere 80. No news about if they had a disco for the reception.

Most Productive: There's a gravestone at Stones Church, Ripon, Halifax that records that Mrs Sarah Crawshaw, who died on Christmas Day in 1844, left an incredible 397 descendants. Imagine trying to remember the birthday list!

Fattest Man: This dubious honour goes to the Rev Joseph Coltman of Beverley, who weighed in at a more-than-portly 43 stones. To get to his pulpit (presumably to preach about loaves and fishes) he had to be propelled up a ramp by two strong men.

Finest Long-Distance Walker: A blistering performance back in 1733 by Foster Powell of Horsforth steals the show here. In just five-and-a-half days he trundled from London to York — and back, the time including his stops.

Most Persistent Yorkshire Driver: Wakefield lady Mrs Miriam Hargrave showed true Yorkshire grit when faced with the daunting prospect of taking her driving test. She failed: 39 times. However, in 1970 she managed to finally tear up her L-Plates at the age of 62.

Most Innovative Playwright: Deciding that a certain William Shakespeare was making life unbearably miserable, Tate Wilkinson, the 18th century manager of the York Theatre, rewrote Hamlet with a happy ending. Old Will must have been turning in his grave.

Taking a Shine: Four teenagers from the Sheffield Citadel Band of the Salvation Army polished 6,780 pairs of shoes (with the owners still wearing them) over an

The Rev Joseph Coltman of Beverley, weighed in at a more-than-portly 43 stones

eight-hour period in February 1982 to raise cash.

Meanest Man: Although some people may think they know differently, the "official" tightest bloke ever was the guy who, when he went out, would press his face into the flour at the top of the bin, and then put his face back into it when he returned. Woe betide anyone who had the temerity to have pinched any. His name? Old John Mealy Face of Topcliffe, born in 1784.

Last Wife Sold in Yorkshire: Now this is bizarre .... A man was charged at Leeds Police Court as recently as 1926 after he decided he would get rid of his wife for the princely sum of £10. Mind you, at Selby in 1862 a man parted with his wife — for just a pint.

Longest Spell in Bed: Lovelorn William Sharp was let down by his fiancée on what was to have been his wedding day and promptly returned home to his farm near Keighley. Many would have simply drowned their sorrows. Not our William, he took himself off to bed and stayed there. For 49 years!

Longest Spell out of Bed: Talk about the opposite to Mr Sharp — Christopher Pivett had the misfortune to have his house accidentally burn down in York in 1756. He died 40 years later having never slept in a bed again. Strange.

Tallest Yorkshireman: The South Skelton iron-ore miner Harry "Alexander" Cooper holds this record (not a tall story) when, during the 19th century he measured 8 feet 7.75 inches, weighing in at 406lbs. Not a man to be trifled with by all acounts, but sadly he was treated as a freak and ended up in circus owner Barnum's Colossal Show.

NATURAL HISTORY

Here in Yorkshire we are blessed with two National Parks in the North Riding — the Yorkshire Dales National Park, and the slightly smaller North York Moors National Park. On top of this there is a small slice of the Peak District National Park that just pops into South Yorkshire, with the oldest nature reserve being the one established at Walton Hall near Wakefield by Charles Waterton.

In recent years the pressure on these has grown enormously with the number of visitors rising every year, although there are still places to go that offer the chance to wander round in peace.

One of Yorkshire's most famous sons, the writer J.B.Priestley, puts it beautifully: "The Dales have never disappointed me," he said.

"I still consider them the finest countryside in Britain, with their magnificent, clean and austere outlines of hill and moor, their charming villages and remote whitewashed farms, their astonishing variety of aspect and appeal, from the high gaunt rocks down to the twinkling rivers."

So much for the poetry, what about the facts and what can you expect to see? Well, the Yorkshire Dales National Park covers an area of 680 square miles, and the North York Moors National Park 553 square miles.

TREES

Largest Forest: The North Riding Forest Park, which makes up part of the Forestry Commission North York Moors Forest District stretches for an awesome 12,220 hectares.

Tallest Tree: A towering lime tree measuring 150ft at Duncombe Park near Helmsley.

Oldest Tree: Should you visit Cowthorpe, near Marston Moor, you will be able to see the dead remains of the famed Cowthorpe Oak which was a mere sapling at the time of the Romans.

FLOWERS
Largest Botanical Garden: The delightful Lister Park in the unlikely location of the middle of Bradford measuring 53 acres.

Rarest Plant: There's a tiny plot — at a highly secret location in the Dales — where the Lady's Slipper Orchid (Cypripedium calceolus) still clings on despite the effort of collectors to grab a specimen.

ANIMALS AND BIRDS
Largest Wild Mammal: That Monarch of the Dales, the Red Deer, can be found in North Yorkshire, while the slightly smaller Roe Deer is a fairly common sight on the moors in West Yorkshire.

Smallest Wild Mammal: The Pigmy Shrew, which is, as the name suggests, tiny!

Largest Bird of Prey: The mighty Goshawk is making inroads into the moorland around West Yorkshire, with a breeding pair being recorded in the late 1990s.

Smallest Bird: This is the tiny Goldcrest which measures just under four inches long when fully grown — so you'll have to keep your eyes peeled if you want to see one.

"HAPPY NOW ?"

The tallest tree

Largest Concentration of Sea Birds: This is at Flamborough and Bempton Cliffs, where the noise can be deafening. Incidentally, Bempton Cliffs provide the only mainland nesting site for Gannets in England.

Largest Roost: Around 250,000 Swallows and Sand Martins take advantage of Fairburn Ings near Pontefract as a handy dropping off point during their autumn migration. There are also the huge flocks of Starlings that descend on Bradford city centre every evening to rest up for the night.

THEATRE, MEDIA, MUSIC
& THE ARTS

THEATRE
Largest Open Air: The one at Scarborough that opened in 1932 housed a stage 182 feet long with a seating capacity of 7,000. Sadly however this has now closed.

Largest: Sheffield Arena is now the proud flagbearer of this title, after its opening on May 31, 1991, with crowds of over 11,000 being catered for. The record for a run is 115,000 visitors for the 12 performances of the Torvill and Dean ice spectacular in 1994. The venue can also be converted for other events such as rock concerts and world championship boxing.

Oldest: Richmond's Georgian Theatre steals the prize here — it is also the second oldest in England, being founded in 1788. Not only that, it is also thought to be the smallest one in Yorkshire, with a capacity of 200.

MUSIC
First Yorkshire Brass Band Competition: Held at the Piece Hall in Halifax more than 100 years ago, where the winners were the Clayton Band.

Most Famous Brass Bands: There can be little doubt that they are the wonderful Brighouse and Rastrick, plus Black Dyke Mills and Grimethorpe.

Most Famous Yorkshire Choir: This would be the Huddersfield Choral Society, who started to harmonise beautifully back in 1832.

Most Famous Song: Our "National" Anthem — On Ilkla Moor Baht 'At, invented (or so it is claimed) by the congregation of a West Riding Chapel after a day-trip to Ilkley.

MEDIA
Oldest Newspaper: The Leeds Mercury, founded in 1718, was later incorporated into the Yorkshire Post, and since 1939 we have been proud to have a smashing morning paper in the county.

Best Magazine: J.B.Priestley wrote the introduction to the first edition of this fine publication. It was started in April 1939 by Editor Harry J. Scott in the front room of his Clapham house with a print run of 4,000 costing £21, with a copy costing 3d. Circulation is now close on 60,000, the largest of any regional journal in the country. And the title? Why, The Dalesman — of course!

First Yorkshire Television Broadcast: The Test at Headingley on Monday July 29, 1968. It was also the first time ITV had covered a Test Match.

First Ilkley Literature Festival: First held in 1973, this now has an excellent reputation for providing a showcase for young writers and established authors.

First Sculpture Park: Yorkshire again leads the way with the opening of the first sculpture park in the country at West Bretton in Wakefield 1977, just off the motorway. Some of the finest works by modern British sculptors can be found in the rolling 260 acres.

BUILDINGS TO BRAG ABOUT

As you would expect, a county the size of Yorkshire has some fascinating, unique and downright odd-looking buildings spread through its broad acres — here's a selection of just some of those that deserve special attention:

Largest House: The ever-imposing Castle Howard, near York. One of the largest frontages of any building in Britain, and the scene-setter for many a film and television programme.

Highest Inhabited Building: This honour goes to Tan Hill, the inn up the Dales where problems getting home due to bad weather must offer one of the very best reasons for staying for that last pint!

First Semi-Detached Houses: Nestling in Arnford, near Hellifield, there's a farmhouse built not as a single building, but as a pair of semis. Constructed around the end of the 17th century, these can still be seen today.

First Roman Fortress: York (or Eboracum as it was then) first came to light in 71AD. Wonder if the parking was any easier back then?

First Norman Castle: York again pips everyone else for this honour, having been knocked-up in a wooden fashion in 1069 for that most famous of French tourists, William the Conqueror. Incidentally, it took just eight days from start to finish — a far cry from the "sorry guv, it's going to take ages" message of today!

First Stone Castle: Richmond is in pole position here, built in 1075.

Oldest Pub: According to church records, it's the Bingley Arms, Bardsey, near Leeds — this has been around since AD905 (when it was called the Priest's Inn), being renovated in 1738. We have been promised they have changed the barrel since then...

Highest Pub: Out of all of Yorkshire's 3,600 inns (the most of any county in England), the Tan Hill beyond Swaledale is the tops at 1,732 feet.

Pubs with Famous Regulars: The Morrit Arms at Gretna Bridge and the Fleece Inn at Northallerton were both haunts of Charles Dickens while penning Nicholas Nickleby; Branwell Brontë had a legendary fondness for the Black Bull in Haworth, while Daniel Defoe wrote part of Robinson Crusoe in the Rose and Crown in Halifax (possibly on a Friday?).

Largest Snow "Castle": As the name suggests this was a strictly winter affair, taking place at Settle in 1886. Some 40 yards in circumference, 15 feet high and crowned by seven turrets, it contained three chambers where 700 youngsters were fed and watered while the frost lasted. Frozen peas, anyone?

Oldest Church Overall: This is St Mary's Bishophill Junior, York, while just nine miles away there's the oldest and most complete Saxon church at Kirk Hammerton. And, continuing the Saxon theme, the oldest tower from that period was built at Bardsey near Leeds.

Highest Parish Church: This honour goes to Greenhow Hill, between Grassington and Pateley Bridge, at 1,300 feet. A clear case of nearer to my God than thee.

First York Minster: King Edwin of Northumbria was baptized by Paulinus on Easter Day in 627AD; a small wooden church was built on the site. Little could any of those present know that their construction would today end up as being the largest Gothic Cathedral in Northern Europe.

Church With The Loftiest Spire: Wakefield Cathedral leads the way with 247 feet.

Church Within A Railway Station: Believe it or not, if you set off for London from Doncaster you will find it on the left hand side facing the engine, directly after leaving Platform 1. Better bear that in mind next time you want to rant and rave at a late train!

Church On The Site Of A Pagan Temple: This unlikely tale involves Goodmanham Church in East Yorkshire. Actually, it's not as bad as it seems, for the Pagan Temple was destroyed by its Priest in AD627 when he turned to Christianity.

Church Trivia: On the subject of churches, there are a number of facts that may bring a smile to your face. For instance, did you know that the largest stained glass window is the Great East Window at York Minster which dates from the 15th century and is about the size of a tennis court, containing around 1,680 feet of glass. York Minster seems to be the place for records: it has fragments of 12th century stained glass contained in one illustration.

Not only that, if you were to seek out the heaviest bell, you would be in the right place as well, with the aptly-named Great Peter, recast in 1926 to give it a weight of 10 tons 16cwt 22lb.

Lewis Carroll always maintained that his Mad March Hare came from inspiration drawn from a stone carving in St Mary's Church in Beverley.

Beverley Minster is the only clock in the world to strike bells in two separate towers, with quarters being struck in the north tower, and hours in the south tower.

The Savile Arms in Thornhill, Dewsbury is the only inn to have part of its property actually within a churchyard. Presumably they serve spirits.

And Finally: How about this for a really confusing bit of writing? At Low Bentham there's an inscription that reads of a woman who became a Husband on her wedding — Anna Husband back in 1683!

TRANSPORT AND COMMUNICATIONS

We can't do with 'em and we can't do it without 'em. Whether it be that annoying tinkling of someone else's (or even worse — yours) mobile phone, or getting stuck on the A1, there's no doubt that we would all be in a bit of a state if we were unable to get around or communicate with each other.

Here are various facts and figures you may not have known about the title-matter of this chapter.

Highest Motorway in Britain: Next time you are on the M62 at Windy Hill in West Yorkshire on the road between us and "them" you may find your car buffeted a bit — don't worry, it's because you are on Windy Hill.

Deepest Roadway Cutting: Not only the lowest in Britain, but the lowest in Europe; it's the M62 again, at the aptly named Deanhead Cutting.

Longest Single-Span Suspension Bridge: Opened by Her Majesty the Queen back in 1981, the Humber Bridge stretches for an incredible 4,626 feet. Meanwhile, the highest single-span suspension bridge is at Deanhead (410 feet) and carries the A6025 over the M62.

First Yorkshire Turnpike Act: This was put down (so to speak) in 1735 and covered the roads from Manchester and Oldham to Saddleworth, and from Rochdale over Blackstone Edge to Halifax and Elland. No doubt this would have been of interest to Dick Turpin if he had been around at this time. The first public stage coach, incidentally, travelled from Dick's last resting place of York to London in 1658, a journey lasting four days. Ouch!

Oldest Toll Bridge: Continuing the pay-as-you-go theme, the oldest toll bridge is at Selby. When it opened to traffic in 1791, a right was granted as a local concession thanks to George III and it applies to this day.

First Tramways: These horse-drawn rail cars first appeared on the streets of Leeds in 1872, superseded by the first electric trams (in Britain) operated by overhead wires some 19 years later, the route being in Leeds on the Sheepscar-Oakwood route.

On The Buses: The first trolley bus was a joint Leeds/Bradford effort, and took place on a trial basis in 1911. It is believed that the first motor bus was used at Todmorden some four years previously to this, although this cannot be confirmed beyond doubt.

Taxi! Bradford again takes its place at the head of the queue with the news that the Northern Motor Cab Company had its first hire in 1908. The city also with Harrogate can boast the first motor agent, one J.E.Tuke who acted as agent for Arnold Motors in 1896. That same year, Mr Tuke became the first to hire out cars on a daily rate.

Taking To The Water: Yorkshire is also one of the end points of the longest possible journey on Britain's canal system: from Bedford on the Great Ouse to Ripon in North Yorkshire, an impressive 415.75 miles with 157 locks to negotiate.

The oldest toll bridge is at Selby

Longest Canal Tunnel: Standedge, Huddersfield Narrow Canal leads the way with 3 miles, 135 yards. At least it did before closure in 1944.

Track Record: Did you know that the first railway to be authorised by an Act of Parliament was the Middleton Railway, Leeds in 1758 as a wooden waggonway?

First Steam-Worked Public Railway: In September 1834, the Leeds and Selby Railway welcomed its first passengers. In a world first, the route involved the use of an engine to draw passengers through Richmond Hill Tunnel.

Highest Summit: The Incline Top on the Battersby to Rosedale mineral line was approximately 1,350 feet above sea level. The highest summit still in use is on the Settle-Carlisle railway at Ais Gill on the border with Cumbria, a towering 1,167 feet. This is also the highest main line railway summit in England.

Highest Stone Viaduct: The dizzying Lockwood that stands at 136 feet on the Huddersfield-Penistone line.

Longest Tunnel: If you don't like being in dark, enclosed spaces, then you had better keep well away from the one at Totley, which weighs in at 3 miles and 950 yards long. This connects Dore and Totley in Yorkshire to Grindleford in Derbyshire. The longest tunnel completely in Yorkshire is Bramhope, 2 miles 241 yards long on the Leeds–Harrogate line.

Deepest Cutting: The one at Chevet, near Wakefield is actually Britain's deepest as well as ours and is almost 100 feet deep. Keep well away from the edge seems to be the wisest advice here.

Longest Straight Stretch Of Track: Another British record for Yorkshire — it's the 18-mile stretch between Barlby and Staddlethorpe on the Selby-Hull line.

Longest Station Seat: Here's not only a British record, but a world record. At sunny Scarborough, there's a continuous wooden seat that runs for 285 feet.

Fastest Diesel: The prototype Inter-City 125 High Speed Train managed 143 miles per hour between Northallerton and Thirsk.

Up, Up And Away: The first balloon flight was undertaken by the very daring Mr Lunardi from Leeds back in 1785.

Slowest Aircraft: This honour goes to the Camco V-liner that clocks up a less than rapid 52 miles per hour. The amphibious plane was built for the Central Manufacturing Company by the Slingsby Aircraft Company at Kirkbymoorside.

Chocs Away: Sir George Cayley completed a 5 foot glider back in 1804. The "Father of Aviation" was born in Scarborough and had a private workshop at Brompton Hall, the family's historical home.

Scarborough's continuous wooden seat that runs for 285 feet...

A would-be flying policeman from Bradford fixed wings to his bike...

First Test Flight Success With A Man-Carrying Glider:
John Appleby had the misfortune to be Sir George's
coachman in 1853 when it was decided that a "volun-
teer" was required to fly across a valley near Brompton
Hall. After a 500 yard nerve-jangling affair, John landed.
You know the next thing he did? He quit — and who can
blame him?

First Flying Club: Yorkshire Light Aeroplane Club takes
the honours having had its first meeting at the Hotel
Metropole in Leeds on September 15, 1909. Things

really took off, so to speak, and within just a month the membership had soared to 200.

If At First You Don't Succeed: "Give up" would appear to be the best advice for Robert Allen, a would-be flying policeman from Bradford. He fixed wings to his bike in the sure belief that if he got up enough speed he must surely take to the air. Sadly, he didn't. Can't blame the lad for trying though.

First Aerodrome: You would hardly believe it today, but Esholt Sewage Works Estate near Rawdon was the site of the Airedale Aerodrome.

WEATHER OR NOT...

Now there are few things that Yorkshire folk like to discuss more than the weather. Is it too hot? Too cold? Will it ever stop raining? Nothing seems to get people talking more than a spell of a particular weather, but it is not always as bad today as it seems as you will now find out.

Severest Winter Within Living Memory: Along with most of the rest of the country, ours came in 1947, known throughout the land as "The Big Freeze". Ours began on February 2nd when the skies darkened and it started to snow — and how — especially over the Pennines.

Worst Floods: The people of Sheffield have the dubious distinction of claiming this record which stretches back to March 12, 1864. 260 people perished after the Dale Dyke Dam near Bradfield shattered after torrential rain letting 114 million cubic feet of water crash down the Loxley and Don Valleys. As well as the human victims, 693 animals died and 100 buildings plus 15 bridges were destroyed. Just 12 years earlier, Holmfirth had suffered when a wall of water nearly six yards high swept down claiming around 100 people and mills, bridges, houses, warehouses and barns.

Heaviest Recorded Annual Rainfall: It is widely thought that Ribblehead earns the damp distinction here. In 1954, when the average rainfall should have been around 70 inches, an incredible 190.5 inches plummeted from the sky, with 5.2 inches falling on just one day in December. Rumours that there must have been test matches being played at Headingley to cause this year's weather have never been discounted.

CHEW ON THIS

Biggest Chippy: Without doubt the most famous fish and chip shop in the world is Harry Ramsden's just by the roundabout at White Cross, Guiseley. Founded back in 1928 (and the original hut is still here to be seen) it now serves well over a million customers a year, not only for takeaways, but in the elegant restaurant where a thirties feel gives even the mushiest of peas a glamorous look. The house record for servings was set in October 1998 when to mark its Diamond Jubilee, Harry's served up 10,182 customers — no doubt helped by the fact that prices for a fish supper were pegged back to 2p, the original prices.

Most Famous Cheese: It used to be Wensleydale, and still is .... Wensleydale, a delicious number from the Hawes Creamery. Incredibly popular, and helped by the animal antics of Wallace and Gromit.

Largest Pie: Since 1778 when a giant pie was made to celebrate King George III's return to sanity, the villagers of Denby Dale have been famed for their baking skills. Their finest effort to date, though, is arguably the six ton pie made in 1964, funded by the sale of the local village hall. With a dish that weighed a ton-and-a-half itself and was 18 feet long and six feet wide, the ingredient list read like this: take ten bullocks, a ton-and-a-half of potatoes, half a ton of flour, five cwt of lard and fifty gallons of gravy. Match that, Delia.

Speaking Of Big: Hosted by the George Neville, newly appointed Archbishop of York, way back in 1464, a feast at Cawood, near Selby, included, among other things, 15,000 birds, 2,000 pigs, 1,000 sheep, 500 deer and 4,000 tarts.

SPORT AND GAMES

CRICKET

Not so much a sport, than a religion, with the most passionate of devotees!

Sadly for those of us afflicted in this part of the world, there has not been that much to cheer about over the last few years with the County Championship evading our men in white so far!

At the time of going to Press, we have grabbed the title 31 times.

However, with players like Darren Gough and Michael Vaughan flying around terrorising batsmen and bowlers alike, there's nothing to stop us from dreaming about glory days returning to their rightful place in the future.

Here then is a roll of honour, with fond thoughts of adding to it as soon as bad light hasn't stopped play again....

County Titles Won: A grand total of 31 — and this is as proud a record as there is anywhere. And on top of this we have been joint champions on a couple of other occasions, plus we have been champs five times for three years in succession. Howzat for a great history?

First Roses Match: Hyde Park Ground, Sheffield, way back in 1849.

Oldest Recorded Clubs In Yorkshire: The elderly Heworth claim the record with a start date of 1784, followed by Hallam in 1796 and Otley in 1820.

Highest Number Of Centuries: The legendary Herbert

Sutcliffe who blasted 112 of them between the years 1919 and 1939, putting opponents to the sword (or rather willow) with great ease.

Highest Score By An Individual In A County Match: One G.H. Hirst hammered the rather bewildered Leicestershire bowlers to all corners of the ground for 341 back in 1905.

Highest Opening Stand: That man Sutcliffe again (313) and Percy Holmes (224 not out) amassed a stunning 555 while taking on those Essex men at Leyton in 1932. Way to go guys!

Top Run-Scorer In One Season: You just can't keep him away! Step forward Mr Sutcliffe with the small matter of 2,883 in 1932, no doubt helped by that huge opening stand. And just for good measure, he's also the highest scoring batsman with the barely credible 38,558 runs, at an average of 50.2 made in 768 completed innings.

Top Wicket-Taker In First Class Cricket: For once old Herbert misses out — for obvious reasons! This one goes to Wilfred Rhodes with 4,187 wickets, averaging 16.71. He's also the top wicket-taker in an individual season with 240 in 1900. And, just for good measure, he's also the oldest chap to appear in a Test Match when he trundled out at Kingston, Jamaica in 1930, aged 52 years and 165 days. And to top the lot, he also holds the record for the greatest number of appearances in County Championship matches, notching up 763. Phew!

Best Bowling: Hedley Verity who grabbed all 10 wickets for just 10 runs against Notts back in 1932. How we could do with him now — he also managed to dispose of 14 Aussies in one day during a 1934 Test Match.

Last Yorkshireman To Take A Test Hat-Trick: The mightily-talented and all-round good bloke, Darren Gough, on the last Ashes Tour.

Largest Crowd For An English Test Match: A bum-numbing 158,000 at Headingley for the match against the Aussies in 1948.

RUGBY LEAGUE

There can be fewer sports in the country that have a more Yorkshire flavour that our own RL! From humble beginnings at The George in Huddersfield, the game has captured the imagination of thousands — Wembley may as well have been moved to Yorkshire when you think of the number of teams from the county have graced the Twin Towers in the hunt for cup glory.

Here then is a quick guide to some of the main facts and figures involving our sides over the years.

Biggest Win: A right trouncing! Huddersfield 142 v Blackpool Gladiators 4, Nov 26, 1994.

Biggest Defeat: Huddersfield claim that most of the tries were all offside... Castleford 94 v Huddersfield 12, Sept 18, 1988.

Biggest Attendance: Time to breathe in a bit — it was a barely believable 102,569 — for the Halifax v Warrington, RL Challenge Cup replay at Odsal Stadium, Bradford, May 5, 1954. Sales figures of Tetley's for the crowd are not, however recorded. More's the shame.

Smallest Attendance: Nowt! During a smallpox outbreak in 1904 there were occasions when the public were barred from attending matches. Not to be sneezed at.

Leading Try-Scorers: During one match for Hull KR against the hapless Brookland, George West ran in an incredible 11 tries. This was achieved on March 4, 1905 and the record for a Yorkshireman — like our George on this day — has not been touched since then.

Leading Season's Try Scorer: Young Albert Rosenfield went over the line for an astonishing 80 tries during the 1913-14 season while playing for Huddersfield. Superb! 'Tis a pity he weren't a Tyke though: he was, of all things, an Aussie. Typical!

Record Number of Points in a Season: 496 (including 36 tries and 194 goals) is the incredible record of Benjamin Lewis Jones for Leeds during the 1956-57 season.

Record Number of Points in a Career: Neil Fox managed a thumping 6,220 of them between the years 1956 and 1979 — and all of them were for clubs within our County boundary — especially the truckload he landed for Wakefield Trinity during his 19-season stay.

Most Capped Yorkshire-Born Players: (Great Britain) Mick Sullivan who plied his trade with Huddersfield, Wigan, St Helens and York grabbed a splendid 46 Test caps, a figure only matched by the man with the 'tache, Gary Schofield, who equalled the feat while playing with two Yorkshire clubs — Hull and Leeds.

Huddersfield's biggest defeat...

Most Championship Titles: Huddersfield and Bradford share this fine honour with a magnificent seven each. No sign of that bald bloke in the black shirt, though! That's Yul Bryner, not the ref. Mind you....?

First Wembley Final featuring a Yorkshire team: Wigan 13, Dewsbury 2, back in 1929. Just as well they are knocking the Twin Towers down, then.

Best Challenge Cup Record: Leeds have so far scooped 11 out of 17 finals.

FOOTBALL

Barnsley: Founded in 1887 and bearing the proud nick-names of the Reds, the Tykes and the Colliers, their best home crowd to date was a massive 40,255 although their smallest home gate is not known.

They have recently been enjoying some of their most successful seasons ever, finishing 19th in the F.A. Premier League during 1997/98, a far cry from the worst league position which was 16th in Division 4 in 1965/66. Their record victory goes back a long way to 1899 when they trounced Loughborough 9-0 although their worst defeat is by the same score against Notts County in 1934. Their record scorer in a career is 122 by E.W. Hine and their record transfer fee spent was £1.5 million for Georgi Hristov from Belgrade in July 1997, while they received £4.25 million for Ashley Ward from Blackburn in January 1999.

Bradford City: The Bantams, as they are known, have been around since 1903 and can boast a record attendance of 39,146 against Burnley in 1911 although there are no figures for their smallest crowd available.

Their record victory is 11-1 against Rotherham United in 1928 and their biggest defeat is 9-1 against Colchester in 1961. Their record goal scorer for a season is David Layne with 36 in the 1961/62 season and their most prolific scorer in a career is Bobby Campbell with 143. The Bantams' record transfer outlay is £1.4 million for David Wetherall in July 1999 and their record transfer received is £2 million from Newcastle United for Des Hamilton.

Grimsby Town: The Mariners were founded in 1878, turning professional in 1890. Their best home crowd is

31,651 for the F.A. Cup Tie against Wolves in February 1937, with their smallest gate just 1,833 against Brentford in 1969. Their best league position is 5th in Division 1 in 1934/35 and their worst 23rd in Division 4 1968/69.

Their record victory is 9-2 against Darwen in 1899 and their record defeat 9-1 against Arsenal in 1931. The record goal scorer for a career is Pat Glover with 180, their record transfer outlay is £500,000 for Lee Ashcroft from Preston in 1998 and the record received is £2 million for John Oster from Everton in 1997.

Halifax Town: Founded in 1911, the Shaymen were in the league until 1992 before relegation, only to see them promoted again in 1998. Their best home crowd is 36,885 against Tottenham Hotspur in the FA.Cup in the Fifties with their worst a meagre 150 against Lincoln City.

Their best league position was 3rd in the old Division 3 and their worst 24th and last in the old Division 4 in 1992 when they were relegated. Their record victory is 7-0 in the FA Cup against Bishop Auckland, and the record defeat is 13-0 away at Stockport in the Thirties.

Albert Valentine, with 34 goals, is the leading scorer for a season while Ernest Dixon with 129 has the most in a Halifax career. Record transfer received is £300,000 from Fulham while the record outlay is £50,000 to Hereford.

Huddersfield Town: Founded in 1908, the Terriers gained election to the league two years later. Playing at the old Leeds Road Ground, they managed a record crowd of 67,037 against Arsenal for an F.A. Cup tie in 1932.

The Terriers' finest hours came in the Twenties when they were one of the powerhouses of the First Division, winning the championship three times in a row and enjoying a record victory of 10-1 against Blackpool in 1930.

Ironically their record defeat is by exactly the same margin, in 1987 against Manchester City in Division 2. Sam Taylor and George Brown hold the record for leading scorers in a season, with 35 each — the best total for a career is shared by George Brown and Jimmy Glazzard with 142 each. £1.2 million was spent on Marcus Stewart, while £2.7 million was received for Andy Booth.

Hull City: The Tigers were formed in 1904, turning professional a year later, moving to their current Boothferry Park Ground in 1946. In 1949, they managed to pull in an incredible crowd of 55,019 for their FA Cup tie with Manchester United — figures are unavailable for their smallest crowd.

A fine 11-1 victory against Carlisle United in 1939 is their record win, while an 8-0 hammering at Wolves in 1911 is a date that no doubt all Tigers' fans would prefer to forget. In the 1932/33 season, Bill McNaughton managed to grab 39 league goals — a record that still stands today and the record number of goals scored during a Hull career is 195, all bagged by Chris Chilton during the Sixties.

Leeds United: Originally called Leeds City, Leeds United turned professional in 1919 with the Whites joining the league the following year. Their record crowd is 57,892 for an FA Cup tie against Sunderland in the Sixties and their worst to date 2,274 against Sheffield United in the

Full Members Cup.

So far their best league position has been that of champions and their worst 18th in Division 2 in the late Forties. The best victory seen at Elland Road is 10-0 in the European Cup while the record defeat is 8-1 away at Stoke in the Thirties.

Peter Lorimer holds the record for Leeds career goals with 238. The record transfer outlay is £4.5 million on Lee Sharpe while £3.5 million was received for Gary Speed.

Middlesborough: The Boro turned professional in 1889, joining the league 10 years later. The best crowd at Ayresome Park was 53,596 against Newcastle in 1949 and the best crowd at their new stadium is 34,687 against Tottenham while the smallest at their new stadium is 9611 against Barnet.

The best league position is 6th in Division 1 in the early Fifties while the worst is 2nd in Division 3 in the late Sixties and the late Eighties. Boro's record win is a 9-0 trouncing at Brighton in 1958 although they lost by the same score to Blackburn in 1954. George Camsell is the record individual season scorer with 59 and record career scorer with 345. The record transfer spent is £7 million to Juventus for Fabrizio Ravanelli but this was dwarfed by the £12 million received from Atletico Madrid for Juninho a year later.

Rotherham United: The Millers have been around since 1925 following the amalgamation of Rotherham Town and Rotherham County. In 1952 they managed to pull in 25,170 for their Division 2 match against Sheffield United.

Their best position in the league to date has been when they came 3rd in Division 2 in the 1954/55 season — and here they were level on points with the champions and runners up. Oldham Athletic were on the wrong end of the Millers' record 8-0 victory in 1947, while Rotherham's grimmest league defeat was an unflattering 11-1 home defeat at the hands of Bradford City in 1928.

Wally Ardron holds the record for a season's scoring with 38, while the best total for a season is 114. Lee Glover and Tony Towner share the honour of being the record signings at £150,000 each, while the record sale is Matt Clarke to Sheffield Wednesday for £325,000.

Scunthorpe United: With one of the most unusual nicknames in football — The Iron — Scunthorpe have been around since turning professional in 1912, having moved in the last few years to Glanford Park on the outskirts of the town. Their record crowd on this ground is 8,775 for their match against Rotherham United in 1989, while their lowest is just 1,524 against Chester in 1997.

In 1962, they managed their best ever finish — fourth in the old Division 2, while 13 years later they ended up at rock bottom, having to apply (successfully) for re-election. The record win is a 9-0 thumping of Boston United in the FA Cup, while the worst defeat is an 8-0 reversal at the hands of Carlisle in 1952. Barrie Thomas is the leading scorer for a season with 31, and the overall top scorer is Steve Cammack with 110. On the financial front, they spent a record £80,000 on Ian Helliwell from York and received £400,000 for Neil Cox from Aston Villa.

Sheffield United: Famously known as one of the oldest league clubs, they have spent 110 years playing professional football at Bramall Lane and their biggest crowd is 68,287 against Leeds in 1936 although their smallest home gate is unknown.

Their best league position was as champions of Division 1 in 1897/98 while their worst was 1st in Division 4 in 1981/82. The Blades' record win is a 10-0 thumping of both Burnley and Port Vale while their record defeat is 13-0 at the hands of Bolton Wanderers. The record goal scorer for a season is Jimmy Dunne with 41 and the record scorer in a career is Harry Johnson with 205.

As for transfers, the record received is £2.75 million for Brian Deane from Leeds United and the record paid is £1.2 million to West Ham for Don Hutchison.

Sheffield Wednesday: Founded in 1867, the Owls have been in the League since 1892 playing in front of their record crowd of 72,841 against Man City in 1934. Like their neighbours the Blades, Wednesday are unsure of their smallest crowd. As of their best league position they have been champions four times so far with their worst position being in Division 3 from 1980 to 1984.

Their record win is 12-0 back in 1891 against Halliwell while their record loss is 10-0 to Aston Villa in 1912. The record goals scored for a team in a season is 106 while their record ever scorer is Andy Wilson with 199. As for transfers, the Owls highest spending was £4.7 million to Celtic for Paolo Di Cannio, while they received £2.65 million from Blackburn for Paul Warhurst.

York City: Having spent 70 years in the league, can boast of playing in front of 28,123 people at their Bootham Crescent ground against Huddersfield in 1938.

However, the Minstermen's lowest crowd is just 1,167 for their match against Northampton in 1981.

Their best league position is 15th in the old Division 2 while their worst is bottom of the old Division 4. The record victory of 9-1 against Southport in 1957 is overshadowed by their 12-0 defeat by Chester in 1936. Their record career scorer is Norman Wilkinson with 127 from 1954 to 1966. Their record transfer spend is £140,000 for Adrian Randall from Burnley while they received £950,000 from Sheffield Wednesday for Richard Crestwell.

CYCLING

With all the wonderful scenery in our county, it is little wonder that cycling is incredibly popular in this part of the world — and we have had some real champions.

First Cyclists' Touring Club: Harrogate, formed way back in 1878.

Arthur Metcalfe: In 1966, Leeds rider Arthur became the first — and only — rider ever to win the British Best All-Rounder Championship against the clock over 50 and 100 miles and the 12 hour distance, and also win the National Amateur Road Race in the same year. For good measure, Arthur also rode in the Tour de France and won the Milk Race in 1964.

Brian Robinson: The Mirfield man became the first Englishman ever to win a stage of the Tour de France in 1958, a feat that he repeated two years later.

Tom Simpson: He has the honour of becoming the first

Englishman ever to wear the Tour's famous yellow jersey as leader in 1962, and in 1965 became the first Englishman ever to win the World Professional Road Race Championship.

Beryl Burton OBE: The Leeds lady has won no less than seven World Championship gold medals. Beryl has also been the British Womens' Best All-Rounder against the clock over 25, 50 and 100 miles no less than 25 times between 1959 and 1983. In 1967 she covered 446.19km in a 12-hour time trial, which was then 9.25km further than the men's record!

In 1972, both Beryl and her daughter Denise became the first ever mother and daughter to compete in the world championship when they were both selected for the British team.

Yvonne McGregor: How about this for class? In 1999, Yvonne won the Women's National 25-mile Championship at Tarleton in Lancashire for the fifth time in six years. The 1999 Men's National 25-mile champ was Chris Newton.

HOCKEY
Oldest club: Halifax, founded in the early 1880s.

Yorkshire Player Capped Most For England: Norman Hughes with 105 — and for good measure he is the ex-England and Great Britain skipper.

Most Capped Player For Yorkshire: David Higham with 202.

FANCY MOVING ONE OF YOUR CAPS -
SO I CAN HAVE A PEG ?

Most capped player for England

SQUASH

First Meeting Of The Yorkshire Squash Rackets Association: This took place on September 2, 1936, and was the key for many a man and woman to lose their breath on the courts.

First League: Seven clubs — Halifax, Sheffield, Harrogate, Hull, Heaton, Huddersfield and Catterick combined in 1961.

First League Competition: Queens won the inaugural competition in January 1961 — a second division was added in 1969, a third in 1970 and a fourth in 1971.

Most Times Capped For England: Ian Robinson grabs this one with 55. Ashley Naylor managed 29 in the Eighties.

Longest Serving President: This honour goes to Mike Grundy who held office from 1962 to 1987.

YACHTING
Oldest Club: The Bridlington-based Royal Yorkshire, founded in 1847.

Highest Water Used: At 1,320 feet above sea level, Fly Flats Reservoir makes a splash here.

Largest Water Used: Grimwith Reservoir, the largest single sheet of water in Yorkshire.

Smallest Water Used: This award goes to Punden Reservoir in Haworth.

HORSE RACING
First Recorded: The Romans who were always fond of a punt or two had us under starter's orders way back in 210 AD. Fancy a fiver each way on Claudius in the 2.15?

First Race-course: At Netherby, near Kirkby Overblow.

Oldest Steeplechase: The famed Kiplingcotes Derby that was first raced in 1619. This marathon trek is still held to this day in the East Riding.

Oldest Classic Horse Race: Our very own St Leger, run at Doncaster in September. First won in 1776 by South Yorkshire's Albaculia.

Heaviest Weight Carried: Would you believe 30 stones? Now that is a handicap. It was in 1788 involving a match between two jockeys at York.

FIELD SPORTS

Love them or loathe them, they have played an integral part in the development of our county's landscape.

Oldest Grouse-Shooting Butts: These are on Rushworth Moor and date back to around 1830.

Oldest Hare-Hunting Pack: A real part of history, this one, it is the Penistone Harriers, dating back to 1260.

Highest Number Of Pheasants Bagged In One Shoot: Avert your eyes, bird-lovers, for it was 7,000 in two days at Warter Priory near York in 1914. Grouse did not exactly have an easy time of things either. Thomas, 6th Baron Walsingham, bagged 1,070 grouse with one gun on August 30, 1988. And it gets worse for our winged chums: between 1867 and 1923 the 2nd Marquis of Ripon bagged 556,813 of game. Bless 'em.

Oldest Hunt: And this is in the country — it's the Sinnington Hunt with their base at Kirkbymoorside.

HANG GLIDING

First Introduced Into Yorkshire: This most dare-devil of pursuits was first spotted in our county around 1976 and there are now more than 150 members of the Dales Club.

Cross Country Flights: There are now several flights of 100 miles or more starting from Wether Fell near Hawes. At one time Peter Hargreaves from Bishop Auckland set a British Open Distance Record of 136 miles to Skegness.

MOTORCYCLING

First Auto Cycle Union: Formed in 1907 as an organisation that was completely separate from the better known Royal Automobile Club — hence the Auto in the title.

Premier Annual Event: Each October sees the running of the Scott Trial at Arkengarthdale, universally recognised as the toughest sporting trial anywhere in the world.

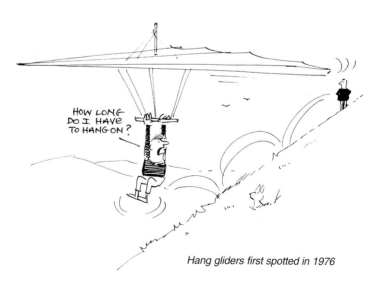

Hang gliders first spotted in 1976

GOLF

Fore!: The Yorkshire Union of Golf Clubs can proudly boast of records dating back to 1894.

Number Of Courses: There are around 160 in our region.

ARCHERY

Who Is William Tell?: A.Webster of Sheffield holds the record for the longest shot with 847 yards, 0 feet, 3 inches. Robin Hood, eat your heart out!

Oldest Archery Club: This is believed to be the one at Ripon which fell into decline, but was put back on target in 1934.

British Record: At what is known as the York Round there are a maximum of 1,296 points to be scored, and at Meriden in 1983, Steven Hallard achieved a mightily impressive 1,296.

SNOOKER

First Maximum Break In The World Championships: Cliff Thorburn of Canada set the snooker world alight when he potted 147 in one go at Sheffield's Crucible Theatre in 1983, thus ensuring his place in the game's history.

World Amateur Break Record: Bradford's own Joe Johnson (later to become a Professional World Champ) holds this proud record with a 140 at Middlesbrough's TUC Club in 1978.

AND FINALLY...

Here's a selection of those snippets of Yorkshire information that may have passed you by in recent years — great for showing off at Pub Quiz Nights!

Through The Looking Glass: It was the village of Croft Spa in North Yorkshire where Lewis Carroll, the local rector's son, took his inspiration for the book Alice in Wonderland.

All Of A Quiver: The oldest sporting contest in the world is the Ancient Scorton Silver Arrow Contest, which dates back to 1673 when 22 archers competed on the village green.

Slow, Slow, Quick: Charlie the tortoise holds the record for being the speediest, who, at Tickhill in 1977 hit top gear to move 18 feet up a 1:12 gradient in just 43.7 seconds. Linford who?

The Write Stuff: Bram Stoker penned his chiller Dracula at Ravenscar, while Charles Kingsley used Malham Cove as a base for his creation The Water Babies.

Up Hill And Down...: Have a guess at how many dales there are in Yorkshire. A hundred or so? 200 maybe? Not a bit of it, there are actually 562 of them — count 'em.

What's In A Name: The vicarage at Marton is the genuine house that Jack built — it was designed by a man called Jack, the builder was a man called Jack, and all of his men were called....er....Jack.

Look Out Below: The deepest well is in St James's Square, Boroughbridge at 265 feet. Built in 1875, it's still a heck of a drop.

Climb Every Mountain: Canon J.R. Wynne-Edwards and D.R. Smith were the first to traverse the Three Peaks (Ingleborough, Whernside and Penyghent) in 1887 in 10 hours.

On Me 'Ead Son: The largest football made is a monster measuring seven feet, nine inches in diameter, and weighing in at 80lb by Mitre Sports of Huddersfield.

No Bones About It: The remains of a hippopotamus have been discovered at Armley, Leeds; rhino, lions and elephants have been found at Kirkdale Cave, Kirkbymoorside; and mammoth and bison at Sewerby, near Bridlington.

Some Bargain: A two-week holiday at Goathland was once a prize on the Nicholas Parsons' quiz show Sale of the Century.

Clucky Character: The largest hen's egg weighed in at 8.5 ounces at Lodge Farm, Kexby Bridge, near York in 1964.

My Kingdom For A...: The tomb of a 15th century knight at a Giggleswick church was opened up, only to discover that there was the skeleton of his horse in there as well.

X Marks The Miss: F.R. Lees, the Temperance candidate for Ripon, is thought to have been the only person never to have scored a single vote when he stood for the 1860 elections. At least he wouldn't drown his sorrows.

Net Results: In 1260, on the banks of Hornsea Mere, two sets of monks (St Mary's, York and Meaux, fought a battle to settle fishing rights. York won.

Narrow Squeak: Dixie, a mouse owned by A.Newton of Sheffield, lived to the ripe old age of just over 6. He passed to that great cheeseboard in the sky in 1981.

Cheers!: Some good news for all of us — Yorkshire has around 3,600 inns, more than any other county in England.

The largest football measured seven feet, nine inches in diameter

OTHER HUMOUR BOOKS FROM DALESMAN

Tales from the Dalesman
£4.99
Packed with wry Yorkshire humour and reprinted in a new format, this selection of humorous tales and observations is taken from Dalesman's extensive archives.

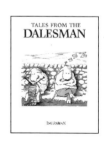

Best Yorkshire Tales
£4.95
A collection of humorous Yorkshire tales — part of a vast stock of humour contributed over a period of more than half a century to the Dalesman.

Yorkshire's Yammer
£4.99
Complete guide to the natural Yorkshire tongue combining dialect and a dictionary of words. Essential reading for dyed-in-the-wool tykes, new settlers or "flummoxed" visitors.

Yorkshire Wit and Wisdom
£3.99
Old Amos has been a regular
and much loved feature of
Dalesman for many years.
Gathered in this book are his
most profound, relevant,
frivolous and amusing
observations.

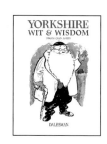

More Yorkshire Wit and Wisdom
£3.99
Further words and illustrations
from that most durable and
amusing of gentleman, guaran-
teed to be greeted with
enthusiasm.

Great Yorkshire Joke Book
£3.99
'There's nowt so funny as foak,
specially wick uns'.
This book catalogues some of
the very best (and worst!) of
Yorkshire humour.

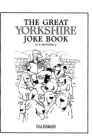

Favourite Yorkshire Humour
£4.95
Selected tales from a fund of favourite stories giving a real insight into the Yorkshire character.

One Dog and his Man
£3.99
A must for dog lovers everywhere, these cartoons capture the amusing relationship between the farmer and his sheepdog. No prizes for guessing who has the upper paw!

**Now available from bookshops or from Dalesman
direct at
Stable Courtyard, Broughton Hall, Skipton,
North Yorkshire BD23 3AZ.**

**Order by phone on: 01756 701381
or fax on 01756 701326
website:www.dalesman.co.uk.**